Island Harbour Village

Denise Crawford

To the people of Island Harbour Village

Acknowledgements

A special thanks to Janet Smith, Gary Smith, Nina Rodiguez, Paula Webster, Parris Webster and Conerjo Rogers. I couldn't do this project without your help.

Content

Welcome to a literary tour of our history, heritage, people, culture, and attractions.

Island Harbour Village consists of three short stories: Island Harbour Village, Two Fishermen and Picks.

Island Harbour Village Heritage

I'm from the picturesque village of Island
Harbour. There has always been a debate about
where Island Harbour got its name from. There
are a couple of stories that have been passed
down through generations by word of mouth
that sound reasonable, but have no records to
prove them.

It is believed that some time long ago, a
group of Irish people were shipwrecked off the
northeastern tip of Anguilla and made it to
shore, and later called the area Ireland Harbour.
Some stayed together, and others mixed with the
African community already inhabiting the
island. Even though there are no official
documents of this, the truth is that, there is a
heritage of people who live in Island Harbour
Village with Irish surnames, mainly Harrigan
and Webster, and claiming to be of Irish descent,
and there is a shipwreck somewhere between
the northeastern part of Anguilla and Scrub
Island.

I believe the story that the village was
originally called Ireland Harbour, and I can
understand the stories about how the name
Ireland became Island. It has been said that it

was difficult for the Africans to say Ireland. Just getting that *Ire* syllable fine-tuned was a vocal challenge, so they omitted *re* and sounded the *I* along with land, and that is how it became, *Island* instead of *Ireland*. It is not uncommon for some words to take on a different pronunciation because some syllables are hard to vocalize. And the other story is that the African misunderstood the Irish and thought they were saying Island, so they pronounced it as they understood it.

Island Harbour is a sleepy fishing village located on the northeastern part of Anguilla. The village has many different communities - some original, and some new ones. Back in the day, it was customary to not build too close to the water because of fear that houses might get blown into the sea by hurricane winds, and the sea blast would damage houses, and too, the sea rocks or coastline is protected by law for the villagers to go fishing and to do other seaside activities. The first communities are The Keys, The Hill (also known as The Webster's Yard), The Bay, The Point and The Broad Path. The Bay is the central part of the village and is also the divide between the African and Irish communities. The Bay, The Hill, The Point and The Keys are predominately Irish. The Broad Path consists of two communities called The Garlin Bottom and Long Bottom, and they are predominately African communities. The Sea Rocks, Harbour Ridge and Captain's Ridge are the new communities, and they are predominantly expat residential communities and villa rentals for tourists. All three of these communities are built along the sea rocks with regards for our fishing tradition and other seaside activities.

The village has always been a place with an interesting past. During the time when the British government commissioned the islands called the St. Kitts-Nevis Association to oversee Anguilla while they were deciding on what to do with the island, the St. Kitts-Nevis Association mistreated Anguillans. The people of Anguilla were not happy, so they got together and planned a revolt to be separated. There was a combination of things that sparked the revolt; but when the British government officially joined Anguilla as part of the St. Kitts-Nevis Association and called it the Associated State of St.Kitts-Nevis-Anguilla, that was the last straw. My favourite story, however is, was when the people of Anguilla requested a wharf to be built *on Anguilla* for the boats to dock, because they didn't have one. Apparently the government of St. Kitts-Nevis made the request to the British government and they sent the funds to build the wharf. The St. Kitts-Nevis Association was at least kind enough to build the wharf and they called it Anguilla Wharf. The only problem was that the wharf was built *on St. Kitts*! Anguillans had had enough and refused to be a part of this association, so they started to revolt.

During the revolt, the British government sent in paratroopers after being told by the prime minister of St. Kitts-Nevis that some Anguillans had guns, mainly those from Island Harbour Village. The village was besieged by paratroopers who built a barrack using sea water on Island Harbour beach, and resided there.

Island Harbour villagers from down in the Webster's Yard to the far end of the Broad Path all took part in the revolt. Some were reprimanded and wounded from being shot by paratroopers. But they fought and stuck to their beliefs that they were no longer going to be mistreated. The British government heard their voices and saw their fight, and allowed the separation. Anguilla's first chief minister is no other than a man from Island Harbour Village, Mr. Ronald Webster! He was one of the main leaders who fought tirelessly to ensure that Anguilla was not going be a part of an association that was mistreating its people. He inspired his people, and his contribution is described as phenomenal. His car licence plates read A 1 – Anguilla number one. He is the first man to represent our tiny nation, and he has been immortalized as the father of Anguilla - the one who gave Anguilla its freedom.

The people of Island Harbour Village are very strong. They are people who have always fought for justice and freedom. The Irish had a long battle with England, as they did not want to be governed by them, and the Africans struggled to escape slavery and to remain on Anguilla. With those two heritages and their history combined, the government of St. Kitts-Nevis didn't stand a chance of winning a fight against them. It was evident as the people of Island Harbour Village stood their grounds and weren't even scared off by Britain sending in paratroopers. These were people who knew about hard times and fighting for justice, and they were not going to be mistreated after finding a place in the world where they could finally be at peace and free to manage their own affairs as a dependent territory. They got what they wanted, and have continued to make large contributions to the running and upkeep of their country.

Culture

Island Harbour Village has an interesting mix of people, and not just by heritage, but also, by the way they keep their traditions alive. The villagers are dedicated, welcoming, and friendly. Anyone who had the pleasure of driving through or stopping off to admire the sea view, with its variety of colourful sailing and fishing boats and a cay in the harbour with a background of sea grape trees and colourful seaside island houses, is almost always greeted with a wave. If you see children in dark green bottoms and light green tops going to or from schools, you'll be sure to get a hello and a wave.

Fishing, food and hang out spots are an integral part of Island Harbour culture. It is common for the villagers to hang out in a shaded area. The villagers have a name for this, 'We just cooling out'.

The main pastimes for men include cooling out under a tree or by the side of the road playing a game of dominoes while discussing boats and fishing. These two topics are usually the main discussions. They also group together in their yards when building their fish pots and boats, and you can find them along the sea rocks with their fishing rod or just the plain fishing line, trying to catch a fish and having a lively discussion. Sometimes while they're fishing along the sea rocks, they make a sea rocks grill using four rocks with a piece of fish pot wire, start a fire and roast the fish that they caught. When the fish are done roasting, they soak them in the sea water for a few seconds to give them a salty taste, and then have a feast.

Women are very traditional as they group together in welfare and domestic affair settings. Their pastimes are cooking, baking, and making their traditional fried fish, Johnny cakes and roasted corn. When there are festivities, events and parties, Island Harbour women still today take pride in setting up an outdoor fireplace to cook on using three rocks placed about three inches apart with firewood between them. They get the fire going, and that is the cooker for anything from steamed fish, stew goat, goat water, stew conch, stew whelks, to frying fish and Johnny cakes. When they are baking, they use an outdoor oven handmade from half of an oil drum with two pieces of steel crisscrossed as a support to hold the baking tray. The baking tray is made from the top or the bottom part of the drum. When in use, the oven is positioned over soft burning coals and a piece of horizontal corrugated zinc is placed on the top with a stronger fire. When checking the Johnny cakes, they use two medium-size solid wooden sticks to lift the corrugated zinc. You have to be strong and make sure that your sticks are strong too, because if one fails, it can get messy. Women have been using these ovens for generations. Also, many women still stick to the tradition of growing their own vegetables, and keeping sheep and goats. In the afternoon when the sun cools down, it is common to see them out on their vegetable grounds planting, weeding or picking their crops. Harvest time is always cause for a get-together, especially if it's corn, because wherever they are roasting, a crowd would surely gather.

The main image that defines Island Harbour Village is when it's a big fishing day and the villagers are waiting for the boats to come in. They sit around on Island Harbour bay under sea grape and coconut trees, on lobster pots, and some lean up against the boats holding their fish buckets and plastic bags held under their arms. Some women hold their children across their hip, while other children run in and out of the sea. Some men and women gather along the wharf to help with the net when the boats come in. The wait is like a community gathering, as everyone from the different communities gets to see one another, and they get the latest about what's going on, and send a hello to their families who weren't present. Some of the conversations are like this.

'Wer Madge, da you dere? Buh I ain see you in a long time. Wer how de chirun and da husband er yours doing?'

'Dem good. Buh how you?'

'Er good. I see ya granddaughter de other day and she getting big; er real young woman she be.'

And the conversation goes on until they hear the sound of a conch shell blowing in the distance, signaling that the fishing boats are coming in. The boats sail close to the sea rocks, blowing the conch shell to alert the villagers who haven't made their way down to the bay to come down because the fish are coming in. When the boats come in everybody scrambles to get their fish. Those who helped with the net, get a share of fish in return for their help. But the gathering doesn't end there, because as soon as they get their fish they all go home to scale and gut them, and then season them with season-all and black pepper, and some would add a hint of fresh crushed garlic. They let that sit for about an hour while they prepare dough for Johnny cakes, get the three rock fireplace cookers going, and warm up the outdoor ovens. Meanwhile, children are out getting sea grape leaves. When the fry up starts, you can hear the fish sizzling in the frying pan and smell the Johnny cakes baking from household to household. It's tradition to have your fish and Johnny cakes served on a sea grape leaf, so they sit around under a tree holding their sea grape leaf waiting for their turn. And that is when the feast starts. Even though every household is having their own fry up some villagers still stop by other households to get an extra meal, because they have to have a taste of everybody's cooking hand.

The most delightful part of Island Harbour Village culture is when the villagers get together because of their love for the sea and what it gives them.

Water Wells

In the past, the village used three main sources of getting water for housework: Big Spring Cave, Junks Hole Well and The Keys Wells.

The name of the Big Spring Cave describes it well - a cave that has a spring. It is where some of our first inhabitants (the Carib and Awarak Indians) spent their time carving many faces into the rocks and on the cave walls, and they probably used it as a source for water. When the villagers discovered it, it was used as their source of water for housework, to water their plants, to get small fresh water fish for their cisterns, and to wash their clothes. Back in the day, it was common to see the villagers washing their clothes in the cave and hanging them out on the trees and rocks outside. It was a spot for socializing, as they would chit chat while washing and would carry on chit chatting while they waited for their clothes to dry. Today it's a heritage site run by Anguilla National Trust, and they offer guided tours. Whether you are passing through the village or staying with us while on holiday it's worth a visit.

The Keys Well is located off the community main road. Because of its location, villagers who had pickup trucks used to drive there and fetch water in buckets, and deliver them to all who needed water. Others who lived closer used to walk home with their buckets full of water on their heads, some holding their bucket and others hands-free. During my childhood, I tried to master taking a bucket of water on my head without holding the bucket, but it seems as though only our parents or grandparents had the ability to accomplish such a skill, because I don't know of any youngsters who were able to do it. Looking back, I can still see those older women making their way through the community with their buckets on their heads. It was skilful and one of my most memorable cultural images.

The Junks Hole Well is located in a nearby area, called Junks Hole. It was mainly used by the villagers in the Broad Path community. At the well was a small house, a water trough, two almond trees and a dry stone wall. The surrounding area was bushes and field land where the villagers kept most of the sheep and goats. Apart from some villagers' daily trips to the well to fill up the water trough for their animals, the journey to Junks Hole Well was a day out, mostly on Saturdays, for the villagers to do their washing during the dry season. On a washing day, adults and children together would head out early in the morning to beat the over head sun, carrying their clothes in washing tubs, bags and in buckets on their heads along a bush path. The children carried what they were able to, which was usually the lunch - Johnny cakes and fried fish. The journey to the well was about thirty to forty minutes, and another twenty minute walk would take you to the Junks Hole beach. Once they arrived, the villagers would bucket the water out of the well, fill up the washing tubs and the adults start hand washing their clothes. The children rinsed, and then hung the clothes along the dry stone wall and on trees and rocks. While the clothes were drying, some adults cooled out under the almond trees and others went salt picking at a salt pond located across from Junks Hole beach, and the children would go to the beach. At the beach, the children would scatter in little groups picking sea grapes and coco plums, and a few boys would climb trees to get coconuts so they could drink coconut water and eat jelly. After their bellies were full with all the local fruit, they would go into the sea and climb on to one another's shoulders jumping off into the water and splashing water into one each other's faces. After they had enough fun, they'd go back to the well and eat their lunch and then get a good body scrub down, hair washed and sea-wear rinsed and hung out to dry. While they waited for the last remaining over head sun to cool down, they all cooled out under the almond trees. During this time, the girls plaited their hair and some of the young boys climbed the almond trees to pick almonds. When the sun had cooled, they would pick up their clothes, fold them and put them in their containers and head home through the bushes singing *'Michael row your boat ashore Halleluiah'*, along the way. They usually arrived home before it got dark. This was a day out the youngsters used to look forward to because it was a fun activity rather than a day out washing clothes.

The village's wells remain active and are still used by a small few. Today, the government supplies water by means of pipes to the village. Water wells were an integral part of our village life, as the need for water extended onto our social life and community togetherness.

Island Harbour Primary School

For many years the children of Island Harbour Village went to the Old East End Primary School. Not only was this an overcrowded one-room school in another village, it was a long distance to walk and was built close to a pond. When it rained, the pond flooded and covered the roads making it impossible for vehicles or pedestrians to pass. The children were unable to get school for days on end, and sometimes even longer after heavy rains during the hurricane season. The barrack that was built by the paratroopers during the Anguilla's Revolution was turned into a school for the children of Island Harbour Village to attend without any hindrance.

Today, Island Harbour Primary School is still the only school on Anguilla that is built on a beach. Because of that, some believe its students were doomed to failure. Island Harbour Primary School has always had the lowest percentage of students in Anguilla to get into high school. It has always been said that the view of the sea with Scilly Cay along with the fishing boats and yachts sailing in and out of the harbour were a distraction and this made it difficult for the children to focus on their lessons. The villagers believed that those who marked the test probably didn't like them, because it made no sense to them that children who were doing well in their lessons throughout the school year were failing the test - not once but two and three times. Even when one of the best educators in the history of Anguilla came in as headmaster, he wasn't able to get students a passing grade. People became so worried about their children's education that they took them out of Island Harbour Primary School and sent them to East End. This school had an average to high percentage of student passing rates. Not only did the people of Island Harbour want to give their children the best possible chance of getting into high school, they wanted to see if being schooled on a beach was the reason they weren't passing the tests.

One year it became so bad that only one person from Island Harbour Primary School passed, and the following year no one passed. That was the end of the grammar school as Anguilla introduced a comprehensive school system that gave the opportunity to children of all abilities to go on to high school at a certain age.

A grammar school is a high school that requires students from primary schools to take a test and pass it before they can attend. At the age of eleven students' educational futures were *determined* by a test. With no other options in Anguilla, failing this test marked the fall of some children, which left many of them feeling not very smart, and who endured a lot of name calling as a result. Children were called dunce, stupid and retard. This system created more feelings of low self-esteem, insecurities and feelings of a failure in our children than the good it did to those who succeeded at it. Nevertheless, this is a good system, but it is only good if there is another option available to students who failed, because not everyone progresses at the same capacity, and when taking a test there are a number of factors that can cause students to fail. Also, to stop a *child* from getting a secondary education because he or she did not get a passing grade on a test only showed how flawed the system was due to its lack of an alternative. A full education should be available to every child until the age of eighteen, and the opportunity for children to flourish academically should not be hindered by a test, especially at such a young age.

Fortunately, some members of government saw that a lot of children were being left behind because of the grammar school system and changed it to a comprehensive system that started in 1986, and it's still the system we use today. I remember the start date well, because I was one of the lucky ones who got into high school the year it was introduced. I was part of the group when no one passed. We had hoped for the best, but we knew we were doomed to fail, because there had been so many before us who didn't pass. We began to accept that this was how it would be for us. But some government members stepped in and saved us from the negative thoughts and the name calling that one endured after failing the test.

By introducing a comprehensive high school, the government not only gave all the children of Anguilla an opportunity to go to high school, but saved Island Harbour Primary School, because after East End Primary School was proven as a way to get into high school, more and more parents started sending their children there, and some still do to this today. If the grammar school system had continued, I don't see how Island Harbour Primary School could have survived.

Maybe there is some truth in the idea that being schooled on a beach presents more distractions than not. But apart from our learning throughout the years that was good, our classrooms weren't built facing the sea. In fact, the only times we saw a view of the sea was during recess and outside activities. Seeing a sea view wasn't anything new to us, because it was part of everyday surroundings, which is why we started to have doubts about why we weren't passing the test. We all had to live with the mystery of why we weren't making it during the grammar school system. Today, the people of Island Harbour Village remain at odds about the whole situation. Was it the sea or did they not like us?

We all are grateful that the government took the initiative and introduced a comprehensive system that gave the children of Island Harbour Village the opportunity to get a full secondary education, who wouldn't have received it under the grammar school system. We have many success stories of students who achieved high academic qualifications from both school systems. The grammar school system affected some of us, but not all of us because we found careers in various fields.

Island Harbour Primary School is still going strong in the same location. Its students have been doing very well in their lessons and they have been winning championship awards in spelling bee competitions. In 2010, the name was changed, and it is now called Vivien Vanterpool Primary School. The school opened in 1971 under his headship. Vanterpool was a great educator who has made a large contribution to academia, and the people of Island Harbour are honoured to have their school named after him.

Religion

For many years, Island Harbour Village had three churches, and now it has two. The villagers practise Christianity, but different denominations. The churches are St. Andrews Anglican, Hill Top Baptist and Island Harbour Baptist.

St. Andrews Anglican Church is the oldest in the village, and is one of Anguilla's historical churches. It was built by the community and its congregation. It still stands out, with its big traditional white and light blue arched wooden doors and windows that shut with a wooden latch. On the outside of the church, the names of those who contributed to building the church are engraved in the wall. The church sits on the end of Clarence Rogers Playing Field. The only drawback is that a church hall has been built next to it and this hall takes away from its scenic beauty. It was a beautiful image when it sat there solo at the end of the village park with a small garden and trees.

The Hilltop Baptist Church is located at the top of a small hill with a view of Island Harbour sea front with Scilly Cay in the distance. It is the village church with a view that attracts members from all over Anguilla. The couple who owned it built this church for the community, and they provided a bus to pick up anyone who wanted to join no matter where on the island they lived. They were active in bringing people together by hosting a lot of different events: beach picnics, Sunday school parties and sport games like rounders and bat and ball to keep the villagers entertained. Even before we had electricity, the Hilltop Baptist Church brought cinema to the village using a generator to power the film projector. The films were shown on Fridays in the church, and a white sheet was hung on the pulpit wall as the screen. When word went around that you could see films in Island Harbour Village, people from all over Anguilla started coming. The crowds got so large that the church couldn't hold them, so they moved and started showing the films in their yard. They have a big yard that extends on to the village main road, so people were scattered everywhere to enjoy an evening out watching a variety of biblical and family drama films, all free of charge. Those were the good old days watching films in a church and an open air setting. Sadly, it went into decline when television came on the island.

These two people practised what they preached. They believed we are all God's people and should live together as one, and they did what they could to bring people together by the way of religious and social entertainment.

The Island Harbour Baptist Church must have had the worst time of all churches in the village. This church was built in the main hub on Island Harbour bay. When it was just us, it was already an issue, so I know it must have been bad when the island started developing. About hundred yards away, there was a beach club and restaurant, and all the fishing boats come in right next to the church. Also, on Sundays, men would be down on the bay getting their boats ready for Sunday Boat Race while others would be setting up for whatever they were selling. While this was going on, you could hear the congregation singing or the preaching of the sermon. But when the boat race was over, people would be hanging out in the churchyard and partying while the evening service was going on. I think they used to shut their windows to keep the sound out, because people get real lively during boat race. They packed up and moved the church to nearby Welches Village. I trust they would worship in peace there, because there aren't any entertainment disruptions at its new location. The remains of the church have been converted into Island Harbour bay public bathrooms.

Even with three churches in the village, there were many villagers who chose another church for worship. Most of the Irish didn't practise

Catholicism, instead, they joined a Seventh-Day Adventist Church located in another village. I always think it funny that most of its men members were fisherman who caught and sold lobsters, crayfish and conch, and never tasted them because their religion forbids them to eat it, but apparently it didn't forbid them selling it to others. Funny how some religions work. Seventh-Day Adventist members were very active in recruiting others to join their church, but some of us like seafood and weren't giving it up, and we liked having Saturdays free to go to in the sea and enjoy seaside grills.

For such a small village, the villagers worship at a few different Christian faiths. Overall, Island Harbour people are very religious. They love going to church, and they take pleasure in instilling the fear of God in their children so they behave well and grow up to be outstanding people.

Men

The men of Island Harbour Village not only love sea life, but are political leaders and business owners - owning businesses both locally and in other parts of the island. They also enjoy boat building, farming and tending to their sheep and goats. They are hard working men with a strong entrepreneurial spirit, who never lose sight of the fact that the sea is their bread and butter. They know when all else fails they can go along the sea rocks and catch a fish to sell or have a meal for the day.

Many fishermen do deep sea fishing, catch lobsters and crayfish, go diving with their fishing guns, fish with their fishing rods, catch fish in fish pots, and pick whelks along the sea rocks. But the most lucrative fishing business is the lobsters and crayfish. No matter what kind of fishing they prefer, they always invest in a few lobster pots to make some real money. Most fishermen sell their fish while others give some away and use the remaining catch of the day for personal use. Fishing is not just a business for some fishermen, but a love for the sport, and the enjoyment of eating a fresh fish steamed in a little butter with onions and peppers, and they would squeeze fresh lime juice over the dish to give it that wake-you-up flavour. Some men love this in the morning with a Johnny cake, and can't function without having this in their stomach to start their day off.

My grandfather Philip Richardson was one of the oldest and main fishermen in the village during his fishing years. He used to catch all the Jacks and Cavalli fish. He did other fishing, but his main love was catching fish with his net. He was like the admiral of the sea, because he could predict a ground sea days before it happened, and he understood the ocean like no other. He always got up by the crack of dawn and drove to the different bays or along the sea rocks looking at the sea for Jacks or Cavallis in the areas where they schooled. Sometimes he would go looking twice a day, and if he saw them in the evening, he would pin them in the net, and the next morning he would complete the catch. Years ago, if he saw a bed of Jacks or Cavallis he would have to drive back home and get his net and some of the other fishermen to go and catch the fish. In modern times, though, he used technology. He used his mobile to call and tell his sons to get the net ready and the other fishermen to get ready because he just saw a bed of Jacks or Cavallis. All who helped pull the net got a share of fish, and remaining fish was loaded on to his pickup truck to sell. When you heard a conch shell blowing from village to village, it was Philip driving around selling Jacks or Cavallis.

Philip created a community effort out of his love for catching fish with his net. He used to organize overnight fishing trips to Dog Island cay with the other local fishermen to go and catch Jacks. The Dog Island fishing trips were always the biggest fishing days, as they used to catch so many fish that boat loads of fish were sent to neighbouring St. Martin to sell. There were other fishermen who used to catch fish with their fishing nets, but my grandfather dominated the trade. He was known as the Jacks and Cavallis man. His legacy lives on because there are a few fishermen, including his sons, who have followed in his footsteps and are carrying on the fishing tradition in the village.

Throughout the years, there had been fishermen who got lost at sea. Most were found alive but, there were unfortunate incidents when some were never found. One of the most recent cases was in 2009 when one morning one of our fishermen went fishing solo. When he didn't return that evening, other fishermen went out looking for him, but they didn't find him. They carried on the search the following day with a helicopter and many more boats, and they found his boat floating in the sea with no one on it. They almost called off the search fearing that something bad had happened, but someone decided to take another look along the area where he sets his fish pots and they found him hanging onto a buoy. When he had been pulling his fish pots onto the boat, he fell overboard and wasn't able to get back on.

The day he came back to us, there was tears of joy and happiness that he was found after spending almost 24 hours in the water. These are survival stories in our village fishing culture that give hope and strength to other fishermen; don't panic and give up if you experience a mishap when out fishing, even if the situation looks wretched. Going fishing alone in a far distance is not a good idea, so hopefully his survival story will help to improve the sport and the trade that defines the most common activity of Island Harbour Village culture.

The village has some of the best boat builders. On Sundays and on public holidays it was customary to have a boat race on Island Harbour bay with all the villagers' sailing boats competing. Many teenage boys also learned the skill of boat building. They made their own hand held sailing boats and swam alongside them as they raced. Boat racing is the national sport of Anguilla, and all villagers' boats compete in the national boat races. The Whip, Wasp and Eagle were the village's original sailing boats - owned by some of its oldest fisherman. All boats have won many boat races in Anguilla. One of the new boats is the UFO that was built and owned by younger fishermen, and is ranked as one of the sailing boats with the most wins in the history of Anguilla's national boat racing competition. There are also a few smaller boats that competed and won many races in the small boat race. Island Harbour men love the sea and their boats, so when they build a boat they build it to sail for the win!

There are also many men who became pilots. It is believed that Island Harbour Village has the most pilots of any village on the island. Tragically, we have lost most of them. The pilots were dedicated men who loved what they did, and sadly some died doing it. These men added a lot to their village heritage.

Women

Island Harbour has some of the strongest and most cultured women in the history of Anguilla. These women worked alongside their men during the Anguilla's Revolution, and they kept their families together when men had to go overseas for work. They are up from the crack of dawn preparing for the day, from tending to their sheep and goats, and preparing breakfast for the household to cleaning their houses and getting their children and grandchildren up and ready for school. These women are the stronghold in their communities, and they don't idle when there is work to be done.

In the past, Island Harbour women weren't just skilled in domestic affairs. They were and are still active in helping their men by selling fish and handling the cash transactions. They also cultivate their land for vegetables, which they use for selling and personal use, and they used to hammer rocks in various small sizes as a means of making money. Men would use a big sledge hammer and break up the rocks on their land into smaller pieces, and then the women would sit under an almond tree in their yard using a big solid rock as the main one to hammer the smaller rocks on. We called this activity 'pound rocks' that was usually done when the children were at school. It was a competitive business and a favourite activity among the children, because each family worked hard and fast to pound as many rocks as possible as when the house builders came to buy, they wanted their heap to be the highest so they could get the sale. I remember the days when we raced home from school so we could start taking rocks onto the heap. From household to household, the boys shoveled the rocks into the buckets and the girls carried them to the heap. When we were finished, we went and looked at one another's heap and stood around arguing over whose heap was the largest.

'Man, our heap bigger den yours.'

'Nah, even a blind man could see dat our heap is de biggest.'

He would suck his teeth (stroops). 'You just wait till I come home from school timorra, n ya guh see who heap is gonna be de biggest'

Island Harbour women raised their children to be hard workers by making them help out alongside them. This activity excited us and motivated our competitive and community spirit.

Some of the village women are also successful in a variety of careers and independent enterprises. Being a mixed breed of

African and Irish, we are usually considered the best looking women on Anguilla!

Ann Victoria Smith, also known as Toata, was a village doctor and mid-wife throughout her life. She delivered most of the children in the village during her lifetime. In respect to her contribution and selfless work, they named the Island Harbour clinic after her, The Ann Victoria Smith Poly Clinic.

For many years, the village had its own library run by Olive Hodge. Olive is a local woman who was active in encouraging children to read, and helping them with their lessons. She was also active in the community by organizing events and offering the grounds of her family home for different events and fun fairs. She has moved on and opened one of the first drug stores on Anguilla, and has been awarded an MBE - an honorary achievement given to someone who has contributed a valuable and outstanding service to their community, by the Queen of England.

Another successful woman is Pam Webster. She was the first young woman from Island Harbour Village to win the Anguilla Queen Show. Representing her island and village was something she took pride in. Pam has always viewed education as the main ingredient for success, so she went on to law school, got her qualifications, returned to Anguilla and opened her own law firm, which has been rated as one of the best in the Caribbean. In 2010, she opened an educational centre in Island Harbour to help children and adults alike who need help with any educational concerns and getting employment. She is also a member of the Arijah Children's Foundation which helps children with disabilities on the island. She is very active in making Island Harbour the village where everyone wants to be on Anguilla, and one day hopes to be an elected member of government to do more.

There were a few more ladies from the village who competed to win the Anguilla Queen Show. It was a long period of time between Pam Webster and the other ladies who competed. During that time, one of our girls competed and represented her village in style. When she stepped out on stage and performed wearing a lobster costume, the crowd went wild. If there had ever been a time when it was said that they cheated someone out of the crown, it was then; they didn't give her the crown, they gave her first runner up. She didn't get the crown officially, but she knew she was Island Harbour Queen, because she represented her village and did a performance to match. Since then, a few more ladies had competed and brought the crown home to the village.

Island Harbour's Momma Gwen, from Gwen's Reggae Grill is one of our heroines. She disregarded all negativity that the location of her restaurant was not a good one, and that no one was going to come to that part of Shoal Bay beach. Not only is her location the most scenic on Shoal Bay beach, it is the coolest on any hot day! Gwen opened her business for her love of cooking local food and the joy of working in hospitality. She used her love and skills and created a business that everyone enjoys. When you have entertainers like Rod Stewart showing up on his yacht and choosing it as the place to spend his day, you know that you've done something right! Gwen sticks to the village traditions and pride by preparing her food from scratch every day. She believes in the old people's motto, 'Nothing like a fresh hot meal to catch ya stomach,' meaning that, treat your stomach well and it will get you up and keep you going. On a Sunday afternoon, you can enjoy live music from the Scratch Band Boys.

From pounding rocks to being crowned Anguilla Queen, the women of Island Harbour Village have taken on many other careers, and have contributed to the life, harmony and colour of their village.

Scrub Island

Scrub Island is located off the eastern tip of Anguilla. The island adopted its name because it is flat and scrubby. There is a rock in the sea that broke away from the main island, that's called Little Scrub. You can see Scrub Island and Little Scrub in the distance from most areas in Island Harbour.

Back in the 80s, there were a small group of people who had leased land and built a little village and an airfield on Scrub and resided there. The village was equipped with residential homes, a small hotel, a shop, a restaurant and a bar. They weren't Anguillans, but they shared in Island Harbour Village life. They used to make regular trips to Island Harbour bay from Scrub to bring their children to school. They knew all the fishermen and most of the villagers, especially the boys and girls who used to swim in the bay out onto their yacht that was moored in the harbour. They use to tell us that whenever we come to Scrub they'd give us a tour around the island, so we used to always look forward to going to there.

When the villagers used to have beach picnics on Scrub, they always came true with their promise and came down to the main beach and took them for a drive around the island in their Safari jeeps. They drove them to see the village, the wharf, airfield, beaches, ponds and wild life. The tour was always exciting as you also see the goats running away from the sound of the jeep and gulls flying over head. But the biggest fascination was the airfield. One time when I was there, I was lucky to see the plane take off on its dirt runway. It was exciting to see. Looking back, it was something you see in movies, when someone is trying to escape from a remote area in a small single engine plane. Those were the good old innocent days when we accepted people at face value because these people had brought some excitement to our village life.

The people of Scrub Island left. They had been taken back to their country. Apparently they were involved in illegal activities and were using the island to conduct their business. Whatever these people were involved in, it doesn't take away from the kindness and friendliness they had shown to us, and the joy and excitement we felt when they came to Island Harbour Village and interacted with us.

Since they left, the island has remained untouched, but the airfield is still there along with the ruins of the village and the jeeps they had. There is also a plane that seemed to have run off the runway into the bushes.

The villagers of Island Harbour still go there and have picnics and visit the ruins and the airfield. It is a beautiful Island, and thanks to these people they have left a little, yet interesting history, and their presence on the island is for us all to admire when visiting.

Island Harbour Village 2014

Today Island Harbour Village has a variety of restaurants, a small hotel, two art galleries, lots of reasonable priced villas, a cave with Anguilla first inhabitants' petroglyphs, picturesque views, and a variety of village events to keep all entertained.

The world famous Smitty's was a beach club and restaurant located on Island Harbour bay. It was once the highlight of the Anguilla's social and entertainment life. The club used to host regular weekend entertainment with different performers and bands. Smitty's was so popular that people used to come from neighbouring St. Martin and spend the weekend just to go. Because of hurricanes, Smitty's has lost its original place on Island Harbour bay. Smitty is a local villager who owned his restaurant of the same name, but at another location not far from where the beach club and restaurant was located. He also runs the only gas station in the village. He is a survivor who has always offered work and entertainment in the village, and you are always welcome to stop off and have a drink and play a game of pool or dominoes.

Another one of our great attractions is Gorgeous Scilly Cay. Tourists and Anguillans alike have the pleasure of a short boat ride to the cay to enjoy a Sunday afternoon of local music and the best grilled lobster, crayfish and chicken on the island. He serves up a mean rum punch that will have your head spinning after a few sips, at least that's the effect it has on me.

For many years Scilly Cay was used by the villagers to have picnics, for the boys and girls to challenge themselves to a swim, and for the young boys to mark as a distance to race their small handheld sailing boats while swimming with them.

I was still in Island Harbour Primary School when a gentleman, his wife and two sons started living in a house at the entrance of the school. During recess we used to see his wife walking along the school grounds on her way to the beach with one child across her hip and holding the other one by his hand. Her husband was never with her, but you were more likely to find him hanging out on the bay with the other local guys. Initially, I didn't know who he was, where he was from, or what his connection to the village was, but later on I found out that he was from the village and had left Anguilla for many years and had now returned. He was always friendly to everyone, and he *loved* complimenting the ladies by calling them gorgeous. He used the word so much that the local guys started calling him gorgeous.

One day word went around the village that 'Gorgeous' was having a barbeque on Scilly Cay. He had organized with one of the fisherman to use their boat to take the people across to the cay. Many villagers went and enjoyed an evening of barbeque chicken served up on sea grape leaves. He carried on having barbeques. The free boat ride and spending the evening partying on the cay must have been the biggest appeal, because more and more people kept coming.

Later, he used his nickname and called his business Gorgeous Scilly Cay. He kept his original theme, though - barbeque served on sea grape leaves and a free boat ride to the cay.

Today, what you see is the creation of what started out as a village get-together and has blossomed into a must-visit when on Anguilla. Gorgeous Scilly Cay is not only an Anguilla's attraction, but an Island Harbour one that was born out of village support and togetherness.

Hibernia, a French restaurant is the longest running fine dining restaurant in the village. Raoul and Mary-Pat the owners, ran the restaurant for a few years in Sandy Ground Village before moving to Island Harbour. They turned one of the first houses that were built in Harbour Ridge community into a restaurant, and it has been running successfully for over twenty years after moving to Island Harbour Village. Hibernia is the Latin and poetic word for Ireland. I guess it made its way home!

Raoul and Mary-Pat have a love for art, so they added an art gallery to their business; today it is called Hibernia Restaurant and Art Gallery. The gallery has a selection of Asian art and jewelry; it's open to the public for all to come by to take a look and make a purchase. The restaurant has been a great addition to the village, because it is rated as one of Anguilla's best and it brings tourists to our village. But their greatest asset is their consistency in all that they do. Raoul runs his kitchen with most of the same staff from the day the restaurant opened and Mary-Pat runs the front the same way. They have being supportive by giving back to Island Harbour Village, which is now their village too.

Greta's is one of the longest running weekend barbeque and fried Johnny cakes businesses in the village. She runs her business out of one of the traditional village houses. It's located about four hundred yards from Island Harbour bay on the sea rocks. Greta created the business to give the villagers somewhere to come and socialize while enjoying a local cook up. She serves up some of the best fry patties with fish you would ever taste!

Everett's Beach Bar is situated in the main hub of Island Harbour bay. Everett, the owner, lived in St. Maarten for many years managing restaurants. He came back home to his village to give the villagers and tourists alike another spot where they can hang out and enjoy a day on the beach admiring the pelicans as they dive in the water to catch fish, and the boats in the harbour with Scilly Cay in the near distance. Its palm trees and sea grape trees make it one of the coolest places on the beach to hang out. He serves a variety of steamed, fried and grilled fish and seafood. If you're visiting and it's one of our famous fishing days, he will serve up the catch of the day prepared village-style. He's all about making his customers happy and ensuring that they enjoy their time at his beach bar. Whether you have lunch or a drink, the cool temperatures and the view will make it worth your time.

Elsa's is a local small restaurant. It was born to give villagers who don't have the time to cook the chance to eat a homemade meal. Elsa, the owner and chef, has worked as a cook for many years in one of the bigger hotels on Anguilla. Her love and expertise is in baking bread and cakes, and cooking local cuisine. She left her job at the hotel for a more rewarding career of cooking food she knows villagers and other Anguillans would love and enjoy. People from other neighboring villages and tourists alike all stop by for a bite to eat.

On de Rocks restaurant is the latest and biggest addition to the village. The piece of land that it's built on is called De Gap. De Gap was an area where some villagers used to cool out, jump off the rocks into the sea, and have parties. The sea water is shallow and it starts out just like a normal beach without the sand. Some of us go there in the sea because it has no sand. If there is one thing that some of us villagers don't like, it is sand. We don't want it to get into our hair because it is difficult to get it out of our tight curls, and we certainly can't go home with it on our feet. Walking into the house with sand on your feet is something you just don't do, because sand gets everywhere and is hard to clean out of the house, or so our parents used to say.

On de Rocks has one of the best locations and views in Island Harbour. It has a two-level dining area, so customers can enjoy the view of Island Harbour bay with Scilly Cay, Arawak Inn and Island Harbour School in the near distance. Its biggest attraction, though, is that it is run by a family of fishermen who offer the lowest prices for lobster and crayfish on the island, so everyone - especially on a Sunday - can stop by and enjoy crayfish for as low as $5.

When I first sat in On de Rocks, I remembered the good old days when we used to jump off the rocks into the sea enjoying our young life without a care in the world. Unfortunately, this old custom no longer exists as the area is now enjoyed in another way. In spite of that, I guess when one sits admiring the view and feels the cool breeze, it has the same effect – enjoying life without a care in the world.

There is an inn and many villas in Island Harbour to choose from - some built along the sea rocks and others built more inland. A number of them offer a sea front view of the village harbour with its colourful boats and Scilly Cay in the near distance, and others have sea front views that extend to the horizon and to Scrub Island.

The Arawak Inn adopted its name from our first inhabitants called the Arawak Indians. Its colourful building is typical local style, which offers a lot of character in reflection of the village. Its restaurant offers Caribbean to international cuisine, and it has a gift shop with a variety of items. As with most businesses and communities, the village never fails in offering a scenic view of its harbour and all its beauty in the near distance.

Harbour View villas is one of our oldest tourist accommodations. It is located in The Bay community on a small hill overlooking the village harbour and the surrounding area. It is a short walk from Island Harbour bay, so if you are staying there it is worth an early morning stroll along the beach to enjoy the fresh clean breeze or to take a swim.

Quixotic Villas are another one of our older villas, which are owned by the couple who started the seaside community called Harbour

Ridge. They started it by building tourist villas along the sea rocks to give guest a view of one of our biggest assets - the seafront view of Island Harbour bay and its surroundings with Scilly Cay and Scrub Island in the distance. Harbour Ridge is a large upscale community of holiday villas and residential homes.

There is also an art gallery on Island Harbour bay that has a selection of paintings with village images and portraits of local people. They also have a café for anyone wanting to have a bite to eat and a drink.

In our communities, during the evening and weekends people get out and start up a grill with fish, chicken and ribs, and a cooler of drinks for a good old fashioned get-together. Island Harbour is a community village, people value togetherness and they keep its spirit alive in every way they can.

In 2009, the village started a festival that takes place during the Easter weekend, called Festival Del Mar. The festival is to celebrate its fishing traditions and culture. It is a full weekend of various sea- related activities, and seafood dishes.

Fishermen compete in a deep-sea fishing tournament and deep-sea fishing weighing contest, while the women are busy competing for an award for the one who cooks the best fish or seafood. Seeing that the festival is all things of the sea, they have a traditional swimming race competition from Island Harbour bay to Scilly Cay and back. This was a favourite of the boys and girls in their younger days, but during the festival everyone can join in and compete and share in the sport. Other activities are the big and small sailing boats, and the young boys with their hand-held boats competing in their separate races for the championship award. There is also a boat race called Sunkist sailing boats. They are not the village traditional sailing boats, but a great and fun addition to the festival.

One of our oldest traditions was to go and fetch soldier crabs for fishing bait and race them as a pastime. In the different communities along the dirt roads, the girls and boys used to race their soldier crabs. The only problem was, when we had to pick them up, as they are quick and would reach for your finger faster than you could blink. I don't know of anyone when I was a youngster who hadn't got bitten by a soldier crab. All the bites we got didn't deter us, though, because it was a fun and exciting sport. During the festival, therefore, we let the soldier crabs entertain our guests with a race. It is fun to see.

While you are enjoying all these different events, you'll be entertained by a variety of live music by our local steel and string bands. But the main highlight of the festival is the variety of fish and seafood and the different traditional cooking styles. You will be spoilt for choice, from local fried Jacks, King fish and Caribbean Butterfish to stew whelks, curry conch, and grilled lobsters and crayfish. And while you are walking along the bay admiring the food and the different events, you'll be sure to hear the slamming of dominoes on a board. The game of dominoes is part of our fishing culture, because the village men play on the bay when they are waiting for the fishing boats to come in. From its first year, the festival has proven to be a success, as people from all over Anguilla came and share in the festival. Each year on, it has become bigger and bigger, and now it's an event not to be missed.

Conclusion

The people of Island Harbour are people of good old-fashioned standards and values who continue to maintain the village vibe of sea life and togetherness with each passing day. We suffered a setback during the grammar school system, but that didn't keep us down, because we've turned out a lot of great citizens who contributed to their country's success in many ways. Our men are dedicated to their sea life along with their other business enterprises and careers, while our women still enjoy having a fry up of fish and Johnny cakes away from their various jobs and careers. The youths are curious and enthusiastic about learning so they can be high achievers. Together, we all are dedicated to community togetherness and keeping our heritage and culture alive for everyone to enjoy.

Thank you for taking this literary tour into our village history, heritage, culture and attractions. We welcome you to visit us and experience our beauty first hand.

Island Harbour Village

Two Fishermen
(Inspired by a true story)

It was day four when Joe and Oscar dropped the wood they were carrying and ran from the bushes to the white sand beach screaming and waving at the single-engine plane as it circled overhead: 'We're here, we're here!' As the tail of the plane and the roaring of the engine faded in the distance, Joe dropped to his knees, and repeatedly hit the sand with his fist. 'Were they looking for us?'

'I don't know,' Oscar said, standing akimbo, looking out across the skies. 'But if they are, they have a funny way of showing it.'

Both men staggered back to the sea grape tree moving their heads from side to side.

The two men had left Island Harbour bay and gone on their regular fishing trip ten miles northwest of Anguilla. Three-quarters of a mile into their journey back, the boat's motor stalled. They took turns and jerked on the pull-cord, but the motor wouldn't start.

Unable to figure out what was wrong with the motor and to call for help, the men grabbed

49

the two sets of oars and rowed the boat until their arms and shoulders were sore. Joe panting from exhaustion turned to Oscar and said, 'what are we going to do now?'

'I don't know. Maybe another boat might pass by and spots us.'

'It's getting late and I'm scared.'

'Let's not panic. All we can do is wait to see if someone come looking for us, or if a boat passes by.'

'It will be dark before anyone noticed us missing.'

'I thought about that because we usually get back between 5 and 6pm. Let's just hope someone come before it gets dark.'

They sat in silence and stared out into the open ocean as the boat drifted into nightfall. Even though Joe was nervous he put on a brave face and said, 'We'll get through the night and start rowing first thing in the morning.'

'That's a plan.' Oscar said. Again he repeatedly jerked on the motor's pull cord, but it didn't budge.

With nothing in sight and in the silence of the dark, they pushed their heads up into the covered bow of the boat and rested.

An hour before dawn, they were awakened by a violent sway of the boat only to realize that they had drifted into choppy waters. As the boat sway and lurch, their worries grew.

When the morning sky lightened, they could see that the current was taking them towards an island in the distance. As they drifted closer, the swells got higher, and the only thing they could see were waves crashing into the rocks along the coastline. They were tossed around and smacked with water, and they yelled out to each other to cling on tight to the boat.

Fearful of being boat-wrecked and thrown onto the rocks along the coastline, they jumped overboard in their clothes and plastic sea-shoes. They paddled, while the waves were shifting them back and forth. A few huge waves broke over their heads causing them to swallow seawater.

Breathing heavily and coughing, the men waited for the waves to subside; then held on to irregular, slightly-sharp-edged rocks, and climbed onto the island.

Suffering only small cuts and scrapes, the men moved feebly to where the seawater didn't spread onto the land. They eased down onto the rocks to catch their breath, when Oscar said, 'thank God we made it onto land.'

'What about the boat?' Joe asked, stifling a cough.

'There is nothing we can do; just be happy that we're alive.'

It was minutes after they sat down, they watched with distress as the brunt of a wave plunged the boat into a reef. Joe screamed out,

'Oh no.' Oscar said nothing. He had given up on the possibility of saving his boat. The waves began breaking into the boat, so it became swamped with water, sinking it. Joe said, 'it's gone; how are we going to get home?'

Oscar repeated, 'just be happy that we're alive.' Adding, 'it couldn't have been us who plunged into the reef.'

Thirsty and exhausted, they walked along the sea rocks testing rockholes in which water collects looking for fresh water, until they found one. The rockhole was wide, but shallow. They scooped out what they could with their bare hands and quickly drank it down.

Feeling slightly energized as they were able to quench their thirst, they walked around the island looking for someone who could help them to get back home, but the island was uninhabited. It was a small flat island, and their guess was that it took over an hour to walk around the whole thing. The earth varied between dirt, sand, and a mix of small flat rocks. The vegetation was dense, consisting of tall trees and thick bushes. Dark brown and light grey lizards crawled around on the ground and trees. There were two beaches – one large and one small. On the large beach there were sea grape and coconut trees, and the small beach had coco plums and more sea grape trees. Along the sea rocks were more rockholes with fresh water. There was no sign that people ever came to the island, and the only thing visible beyond the sea was the horizon.

After walking around the island, the two men went on the large beach and decided to stay there, thinking it was the best place to be if they were going to be found. They went down to the rough sea-shore and walked back and forth, while slightly kicking their feet into the water.

As the gleaming sun got over head, Oscar said, 'I'm going to take off my shirt and pants and put them on the rocks to dry.'

'Don't you want to wait here to see if a boat comes by?' Joe asked.

'Yes, but with this rough sea, I doubt it.' Oscar replied. 'And the sun is burning my face; it's probably red like a lobster.'

Joe turned and pointed. 'Why don't you put your clothes on the sea grape tree to dry? It's closer.'

'The sun looks brighter on the rocks.'

Oscar strolled to the rocks. He reached into his deep pants pocket to take out his pocket knife that he always carried, and pulled out a soaked small box of matches along with it. He held it in his hand and thought, if they're any good when they dry, they could be useful. He took them out of the box and placed them along with his clothes on the rocks; he then went under a sea grape tree with big drooped limbs and gathered leaves to sit on.

A half hour later, he called out to Joe and told him to come up and cool out, the sun was hot. Joe continued to pace back and forth along the shore ignoring Oscar. Oscar started walking down towards Joe, who then turned and saw him coming, and walked towards the sea rocks and put his clothes to dry. Joe then dragged his feet over to a coconut tree and sat in silence with a pout looking out to sea. Meanwhile, Oscar stood ten feet across from him leaned up against the limb of the sea grape tree with his arms folded. The remainder of the day, both men stayed in their spots wearing only their boxer shorts, forehead frowned listening to the crashing waves as they stared out to sea.

In the evening while putting on their clothes, Joe's belly started growling. Oscar looked as he wrestled his way into his shirt, and when his head emerged Oscar said, 'The sun is going down and I don't feel like going....'

Joe interrupted, 'My belly might be growling, but I don't feel hungry; I'm too worried to eat.'

'I guess it is just as well, because I was going to say that I don't feel like going to look for something to eat; I don't want night to catch me in these bushes or on the sea rocks.'

They both sat and watched the sun set, until the sky turned dark. They then lay back in silence under the sea grape tree in pure darkness that felt like a shutter clamped down onto their faces, before they fell asleep.

Joe was a vigorous young fellow of twenty-two who had just started a new life. He was of dark-brown complexion with a wiry frame. He wore a medium-length afro, and he always carried a pick comb in his back pocket. Oscar, who was thirty-one years his senior, had been a fisherman all his life. He was of light complexion, tall, medium body frame with salt and pepper curly hair that he hid with a cap. They were fond of deep sea fishing, especially Joe, because he liked reeling in those big fish and bragging about it. Oscar had a small fishing business and Joe was his new helper of six months.

The following day when they opened their eyes the water had calmed down, and they saw something that appeared to be a yacht sailing along the horizon. Joe got up and ran down to the shoreline waving and screaming, 'We're over here. We're over here.'

'I don't believe they can hear you, son,' Oscar said jokingly.

Joe walked back to the sea grape tree and stood shoulders slumped, and his eyes filled with tears. 'I want to go home, I have to go home; I know my girlfriend Mary is worried sick about me. She's pregnant and I'm worried this news is going to upset her more than she needs right now.'

Oscar put his hand on Joe's shoulder. 'I know your worries man, my wife Barbara and two daughters have to be worried about me too. You know, last night when we were lying down, I was thinking of how much I wanted my first child to be a boy. I wanted to take him fishing with me and if she was a boy he might have been here with me and I thought about the extra worry it would have caused my wife. Perhaps it's just as well I never had a son.

'I don't know what I want, but I just want to get home to Mary,' Joe said mournfully. 'She moved out from her mother's house in Welches to come and live with me to start our new life together, and now she is there all alone worrying.'

'I'm sure we're going to get home.'

'But there is no sign that anyone comes here,' Joe said drying his eyes on the sleeves of his shirt. 'The only thing that comes to this island is night and day.'

'I am sure someone comes to this island at some point.'

Joe moved his hands and pointed. 'Look around, the only thing visible is the horizon.'

Oscar patted Joe on his shoulder. 'Calm down son, I believe everything is going to be alright. All we can do now is hope for the best. Put your shoes on and let's go and get some plums, I'm starving.'

Joe pulled away. 'I'm not moving from here because if anyone comes by and we are in the bushes who's going to be here?'

'But we are on this island together, so it is only fair that we stick together.'

'Yes, we should, but what if someone comes to this part of the island and no one is here?' Joe said, walking toward the coconut tree. 'It's my girlfriend I am worried about. She needs me home.'

Oscar rolled his eyes. 'So you coming or not?'

Joe sat on the sand with his knees bent, leaned up against the coconut tree in a sulky pout staring out at the horizon. Oscar looked at him and shook his head, then left and went into the bushes mumbling to himself, 'this boy is really something else, he's acting as though if a boat comes and I'm on the other beach he'll leave me here by myself.'

Oscar came back about a half hour later and Joe was still in the same position. He walked over to the coconut tree holding the coco plums in the shirt he was wearing. 'You know we haven't been here that long and I am sure people are out everywhere looking for us.'

Joe tapped his fingers on his knee. 'I know, but we don't know where we are and they don't either, so we both are going to die on this island before anyone gets here.'

Oscar took a step closer and said, 'look man, hope is our only friend, so let not lose him with talk about dying.'

Joe looked at him and said nothing.

'I always carry a pocket knife, so we have that; and there is fresh water in the rock holes. There is a lot on the island to keep us going,' Oscar claimed optimistically as he took the box of matches from his pocket and waved it in Joe's face. 'And I found these in my pants pocket; it will last for days.'

'What's going to happen when the matches run out?'

'We'll rub two rocks together.'

'Does that really work?'Joe asked.

'I guess we'll see if it comes to that. Come on, have some plums.'

Both men sat under the coconut tree and started eating. 'Boy, these plums make your mouth feel tight,' Joe said frowningly.

'My mouth feels tight too, but plums always do this.'

'Let's get some sea grape leaves,' Joe said. 'I need some water to drink to help wash this taste out.'

They picked a few grape leaves and folded them in a scoop, and went to a rockhole and scooped water out, drinking it from the grape leaf.

'I'm going on the sea rocks to see if I find some whelks or something, so I don't have to eat anymore of dem sour things for the rest of the day,' Joe said.

'It's a pity there aren't any grapes on the trees.'

'You know, some trees don't grow any, and some of them can be sour too,' Joe said, as they walked back to the beach.

'This is very true.'

'Ya coming with me to look for some whelks?'

'You go; I did my job already.'

Back on the beach, Joe rolled up his pants to his knees, put on his plastic sea shoes, and went along the sea rocks. Oscar took his shirt off and rested it on a grape tree and cracked open a couple of dry coconuts that were lying on the sand to get the jelly, but it had turned dark grey. He thought that his efforts would not go to waste because he would use the husks from the shell to help light the fire to roast whelks, if Joe was lucky enough to find any. He sat down and thought about the fact that it was the first time since he had been married that he didn't cruise in to the harbour and see Barbara on the beach waiting for him. His face was becoming flushed, as he thought about how the other women who were waiting would have went home with their men leaving his Barbara there wondering where he was until she became worried. His thoughts were making him heavy-hearted, but they were interrupted when he saw Joe making his way back holding his shirt in his hand. He got up and went to meet him. Joe had a good amount of whelks in his shirt. He told Oscar that he saw garfish swimming around in the water and how he wished he had a line to catch some. They walked back to the coconut tree and he put the whelks on some sea grape leaves in the shade, and he rinsed his shirt and put it to dry. He then lay down, closed his eyes and started thinking about what Oscar had said about hope being your friend; he hoped and hoped until he dozed off. Oscar sat across from him and watched fish that had swum close to the surf jumping around in the water and thought how he wished there was a way he could tell Barbara he was alive.

At the end of the day they roasted the whelks on the sea rocks, and sat down under the coconut tree with the whelks on a sea grape leaves and started eating.

'Joe,' Oscar said. 'Do you remember when that guy went to tend to his sheep in the bushes close to Captain Bay and didn't come back and your brother Jimmy went out with his lamp torch looking for him, and he and others searched and searched until they found him?'

What guy?' Joe asked as he tried to pick the whelk out of the shell with a piece of stick.

'Man he's from somewhere up in the Broad Path,' Oscar replied.

'Where up in the Broad Path?'

'Garlin Bottom I think,' Oscar said. 'Maybe you were too young to remember, but I am saying this because I know Jimmy is out there looking for us and he'll search until he finds us.'

'I know he is looking for us, but I hope he is taking care of Mary because she needs the care.'

'You know Jimmy is a good man and he going to make sure everyone is well.'

'But what happened to that guy, how did he get lost?' Joe asked.

'I think when they found him he said that he couldn't remember how to get back home so he sat under a tree waiting for someone to find him there.'

'You mean his head turn?'

'Something like that, because he said he didn't know where he was.'

'That must be tough not remembering where you are.'

'One whelk left; do you want it?' Oscar asked.

'I'm good.'

'Well I'll eat it then.'

'Did he go by himself and tend to his sheep after that?'

'To be honest, I don't know, because them people up in the Broad Path don't tell us down in the Webster's yard what's going on,' Oscar said. 'But I heard his parents were embarrassed.'

'Embarrassed about what?'

'People were saying his head wasn't good, and they were making fun about it. But this was only after they found him, though.'

Joe leaned back with his elbows turned downward into the sand and knees bent. 'You know I used to have a side-ting from up in the Broad Path while I was with Mary, but when Mary got pregnant she dumped me.'

'I hear some of the boys on the bay talking about it one day.'

'But my heart belongs only to Mary now,' Joe said with a grin.

'I know, you don't need to tell me that,' Oscar said, thinking that if they get off the island alive he would one day tell the boys for a laugh how Joe was teary eyed and all he wanted was his Mary.

Joe stood up, yawned, and stretched his arm. 'It gets dark here quick; I think I'm going to shut my eyes now.'

'Okay,' Oscar said. 'I'll stay up for a while and watch the stars and see if any fall, so I can make a wish before I shut my eyes, too.'

During the night it rained, and both men kept moving around and pulling their shirt over their heads as the water dripped from the sea grape leaves on them.

The next morning when they woke up Oscar asked Joe to climb the coconut tree and get some branches so he could make a shed, because he didn't know how long they were going to be on the island, and water dripping on you was no fun when a man was sleeping. 'I'll climb the tree and I'll go with you to get plums,' Joe said.

'You're in a good mood this morning.'

'When I was finally able to get some sleep I had a dream and Mary was in it and she's okay; we're going to be together soon. I feel someone is going to take me home to her, maybe today.'

'That is a good dream; I hope we get off this island soon. Now, get up into the tree.'

Joe grabbed the trunk with both hands and pushed down on it with his feet, and started climbing. Oscar looked up as Joe's wiry frame reached to the branches. Joe took a deep breath and then glanced down and said, 'Step back, I'm ready to break off the branches.' Oscar stepped back and looked up with his hands on his hip as Joe pulled and wriggled the branches until they fell to the ground. He called out to Oscar. 'I'm going pick some coconuts, so continue to stay out the way.' He twisted and twisted the coconuts until they came off the stem. Joe then slowly made his way down the trunk. He stepped to help pick up the coconuts and swayed a little, so he sat down. Oscar cracked open a coconut and said, 'Drink this, it will make you feel better.' Joe drank it down then rested his head on the coconut tree trunk and took a breather.

When he felt better, they both started walking to the other beach. Halfway to the beach, they heard a motor. Joe ran, clearing the bushes out of his way, leaving Oscar behind trying to catch up with him. As he got closer the sound of the motor got louder. He arrived on the beach; it was a yacht. He started waving and screaming, 'We are lost! Come and get us!' Oscar joined him screaming the same thing. Both men were on the beach standing in the shallow part of the water when the boat changed direction and didn't come to the island. Joe started going further out into the water shouting, 'Come back, Mary said that I would be found today, she needs me to come home. Come back, where are you going?'

Oscar went behind him and pulled him back ashore and said, 'Maybe they'll tell someone they saw us.'

Joe lay on the shoreline moaning. 'Today was the day.'

Oscar grabbed him by his underarm and said. 'Sit up man. If they turned back like that, they probably think we're buccaneers.'

'*Buccaneers*, man no one says buccaneers no more, it's pirates.'

Oscar sat next to him. 'Pirates, buccaneers, whatever they say these days, you need to look at the bright side, at least we know that people come to the island so take your dream as your first sign that we are going to be found and you'll be home soon with Mary.'

'But today was the day I was going to go home,' Joe murmured.

Oscar stood up and said, 'Come on man, get on your feet and let's get some plums to tight up our mouth again.'

Joe stood up and looked out at the yacht as it sped on the water until it was no longer visible. Then both men went and picked coco plums and headed back to the large beach. They put their clothes to dry, and sat on the sand eating coco plum and coconut juice and jelly for breakfast, and watched as an aircraft left a white trail of smoke in the skies all the way to the horizon. Joe thought, if only that plane could have seen us.

About an hour after breakfast, Oscar was confined to the bushes for the better part of the day. He believed the fresh coconut jelly did not agree with his belly. This made Joe laugh seeing Oscar making a run to the bushes in short intervals.

Later on in the day when he felt better, he and Joe started placing the coconut branches around the sea grape tree where they slept when Joe said, 'What if we break off a stick from a tree and make a rod?'

'But we still need a line and a hook. Where we gonna get them?'

Joe stood still holding a branch in his hand, and then said, 'I'll cut off one of my pants legs from the knee and then cut it into long thin pieces and tie them together.'

'Sound good. And you'll have to put small rocks for the cloth to sink. You still need a hook.'

'And ya gonna say I'll need bait too.'

'That is not a problem because you can always use plums.'

'You think fish would bit on dem sour things?'

Oscar grabbed the last branch and looked at Joe. 'The most important thing here is a hook and we don't have one.'

'Man it hurts me to see dem gars and I can't catch a few to eat.'

'It hurts me too, but what can we do.'

Joe stood silent for a moment. 'Aah, I know what; I'm going to make a spear.'

'You think you can catch a gar with a spear?'

'Why-yes; if I try.'

Oscar stopped for a minute and looked at Joe. 'Do you really think you could stab such a long thin fish with a spear?'

'I don't see why I can't if I try.'

'Man, from the minute you try, dem gars would run away and you won't see them again,' Oscar exclaimed. 'But we can still make one and try.'

Joe didn't like what he was hearing so he turned away and said, 'I'm going to look for some whelks to eat before it gets dark; ya coming?'

'Give me a minute to place this branch good so it doesn't come down on our heads when we're sleeping.'

They scanned the rocks along the water for over an hour, and they found a measly seven small whelks. They gathered wood and placed rocks around it under the coconut tree and roasted the whelks. They put their clothes on, and Joe told Oscar he can have four whelks and he'd have three, because he needed more food than him. While eating, Oscar said, 'No more coconuts for me.'

Joe cackled. 'Yes, eat more, I want to see you squeezing your legs and making a run for the bushes like that again. It was too funny.'

Oscar looked at him and smiled. He was happy to see Joe laughing.

'Oscar,' Joe called. 'What we gonna do for something to eat if we can't find any whelks, and can't fish?' 'You see we just eat them whelks in two seconds, and I could eat more.'

'I said we're going to make a spear.'

'But you said I can't catch a gar with it.'

'Yes, but we can look for other fish,' Oscar said. 'Also, we don't know how long we going to be here, so we have to be prepared that if things get worse, we may have to do something. Maybe roast lizards.'

Joe frowned. 'I ain't eating dem things. I'll starve first.'

'Man, when people get desperate and hungry they'll eat anything. I heard tales about people eating their own flesh to survive when they were lost at sea.'

'This story is giving me a bad feeling in my stomach. I think I'm gonna shut my eyes.'

'Okay,' Oscar said. 'Tomorrow we'll make a spear.'

The next morning they awoke to the sunny skies and calm waters. Joe picked up some small smooth flat rocks and walked down to the water where he threw them one at a time, and watched as they bounced off the surface of the water. When he was finished, he walked back to the sea grape tree where Oscar was sitting and said, 'What if we build something like a raft? I'm sure there is a main island somewhere close, and yesterday there was that boat; surely it came from somewhere close.'

'That might be true, but we don't want to be drifting on a wood not knowing where we going. I thought we were going to make a spear.'

'Forget about the spear,' Joe said abruptly. 'But if we start early in the morning we have a whole day and I am sure it would get us somewhere.'

'I don't know these waters.'

'So we are not going to even try to at least see what's beyond the horizon? What about hoping for the best?'

Oscar got up and looked out at the horizon wondering which direction they would go in. 'I guess we have to try.' He pointed. 'If we drift in the same direction as the yacht someone might be out fishing and might spot us.'

'Okay,' Joe said. 'So we'll spend today gathering wood?'

'Yes, that is the job for today.'

'Maybe we should go and dive where the boat sank and try to rip off the board.'

'No.' Oscar said. 'Board swells in water and we won't be able to get any to rip off that easily.'

'What about the oars?' Joe asked. 'We need them.'

'To be honest I don't think I have the energy to hold my breath under water. And we don't know if there are sharks around these waters.'

'If that's how you feel,' Joe said, thinking nothing is going to kill his spirit of trying to get off this island to be with Mary, and he ain't eating any lizards.

'We can use sticks for oars, you know,' Oscar said.

The men spent the better part of day in the bushes breaking off tree limbs with their hands and feet. When they thought they had enough wood, Joe climbed a coconut tree for branches. They both sat in the cool and peeled the green part of leaves from the coconut branch, and the bark off the wood, to tie the raft together. At the end of the day they laid out the wood, but they needed more so they both could fit on the raft.

That night Joe's thoughts made him restless; he wanted the night to be over so he could get up and start on the raft so it would be ready for the following day.

It must have been nine o'clock the next morning when both men were carrying more wood when the plane had circled over the island. Joe stood at the sea grape and looked at Oscar. 'If the raft was built we would've been on our way, and the plane would've spotted us on the water.'

'Maybe,' Oscar said. 'Now, come on and let's go and pick up the wood we've dropped, so we can finish building the raft.'

Joe raised a clenched fist. 'When they come back, we are going to be sailing on our raft!'

They gathered all the wood they could find. They tied many pieces of bark and coconut leaves to the wood. It took most of the day to put it together, and they tested it in the water to make sure it floated. They sat on the beach watching their creation of different size pieces of wood tied together that resembled a raft, on the sand. Joe was pleased and said, 'It will get us somewhere!'

Oscar drew his brows together, strokes his chin, and said nothing.

Joe said, 'You know what, I'm going to climb the tree and get some coconuts. I'm hungry and I don't want to feel weak tomorrow.'

'I don't feel hungry, but I'll get some coco plums because I need my energy, too.' Oscar got up and went to the other beach.

The following morning when Joe opened his eyes, Oscar was standing with his arms folded staring at the sea. Joe stretched his body and said, 'Today is the day.'

Oscar turned and said in a somber voice, 'You sure you want to drift on a raft not knowing where we're going? Do you think this is a good idea?'

'Why-yes; we have to try something to get off this island.'

'What if the raft falls apart, and we're out in the middle of the ocean?'

'I understand your worries, but we need to use our friend hope and hope for the best, and hope that we get home safe; we need hope now more than ever.

Oscar interlocked his fingers, stretched his arms out, and cracked his knuckles, and said, 'Okay, let's go.'

They picked up the raft and started walking. Oscar's heart started racing. 'Let's stop for a minute,' he said and he sat down on the sand with his head down.

Joe asked, 'What's wrong?'

'I need a minute. Why don't you get a sharp piece of stick and write on the coconut tree trunk: Oscar and Joe were here and left on a raft.'

Joe stood beside him. 'You okay?'

'Just go, and when you come back we'll leave.'

Joe walked to the coconut tree looking back at Oscar and wondered what had taken hold of him. He wrote on the coconut tree. He went back, and they both grabbed the raft. While dragging it down to the sea to make a go for it, they heard 'brrrrr'. Not able to make out where the sound was coming from, both men stood still on the beach holding the raft, heads turning from side to side. When it became clearer that the sound was close, and was coming from around the island to where they were, they dropped the raft and ran down to the edge of the water. It was a fishing boat and the men started waving. The boat had three men who appeared to be fishermen and they came into the beach. Joe ran through water, held on to the boat and said, 'We are lost, we don't know where we are.' The men started speaking in another language and looking at each other.

'You don't speak English?' Joe asked.

'No Ingles, Espaniol,' one of the men said.

Oscar came and said, 'We are lost, we are from Anguilla.'

'Aah anguila.' The men on the boat looked at each other and started speaking.

Joe and Oscar can hear them saying anguila. This made Joe and Oscar happy because they knew that the men had heard about them being lost at sea.

Joe said, 'You can take us to Anguilla or where ever you're from, but please get us off this island.'

The men looked at each other and then at Oscar and Joe and said, 'No comprendo Ingles.'

Joe pointed to Oscar and himself, and then inside the boat. The men looked at each other and pointed to Joe and Oscar and to the inside of the boat and said, 'Aah.' Joe and Oscar both nodded their heads. And the men did the come gesture with their hands. They pointed west and said San Pueblo. Oscar said, 'Aah.' He then said to Joe, 'We've drifted west about 50 miles - a long way from home.'

Joe said, 'I know, but it doesn't matter because these men are going to help us get back home,' and he climbed up onto the boat.

Oscar tried to climb onto the boat but he fell back into the sea. Joe and one of the men helped him up onto the boat, and then they headed to where the men were going to take them.

As the boat cruised away from the beach Oscar looked back at the raft lying on the beach with a smile of relief. Joe looked straight ahead over the bow of the boat. The boat ride took over an hour to get to the main island.

When they got to the Island, before Joe and Oscar got out of the boat the men said something to them in Spanish, and Oscar said, 'We want the police.' The men said, 'Policia.' Joe and Oscar said, 'Yes,' nodding their heads. Joe and Oscar jumped out of the boat and helped the men pulled their boat ashore on a small beach that only had a few other fishing boats. The men had a pick-up truck parked on the beach; Joe and

Oscar sat in the back with one of the other fishermen on the drive to the police station.

At the police station, the fisherman who sat with them in the back of the pick-up truck went in and explained to the police where they found the men. No one spoke a work of English, so they had to call in someone to translate. Joe and Oscar walked back to the pickup truck with the fisherman, and shook their hands and thanked them. Then they went back into the police station and waited.

When they met with the translator, they explained the situation. The translator explained to them that they were found on Piso Island, an island of San Pueblo. They explained to the men that the fishermen who found them said that you both kept saying anguila, but they didn't know why, because you didn't have any fish and they didn't have anguila. Both men smiled at the confusion that the name Anguilla is Spanish for the fish eel. Then the authorities in San Pueblo called the authorities in Anguilla, and a private plane was sent to collect them.

From the skies, before the plane touched down on the airport in Anguilla, it was dark with small heads. Joe looked at Oscar who was sitting next to him. 'Thanks for helping me keep it together and telling me about hope, because after you said hope is our friend and not to lose him I felt better.'

'No problem man, I had my moments too. Your fearless and determined spirit is really something. I guess we all have our strengths and weaknesses, because I was panicking about having to drift on the raft; I wanted to wait until someone came and found us on the island.'

Joe put his arm on his shoulder. 'Well it worked out that way in the end. We're home now.'

When the men stepped off the plane, the crowds were lined up along the terminal fence clapping, screaming, and waving. There were faces of joy and faces with tears, but the most emotional people were the two men as they barely held the heads up to look at the crowds of people and wave because they didn't want them to see their tears. They passed through immigration, and the only people allowed in were a family member for both men. Oscar's oldest daughter and Joe's brother Jimmy came. When they got outside the airport terminal the police had to hold the crowds back because everyone wanted to get close to the men to express their joy that they were back safe, because they had given up hope of them being found alive.

Joe was driven to the hospital and Oscar was taken home where his wife was waiting for him. She had been too emotional to come to the airport. When he walked into the house she sat on the couch with tears running down her face.

He sat next to her and put his arm around her shoulder while other family members looked on with tears and smiles of relief. Joe arrived at the hospital where Mary had given birth early by caesarean. He went and sat by her bedside and held her hand and said, 'Mary I'm back,' with tears running down his face, but she was asleep. The doctor took him to the newborn's room and he stood over his son and smoothed down his soft baby curls with his index finger, and said, 'I met a new friend and he brought me home to you. I hope your mother doesn't mind if I call you Hope.'

The end

Picks

Aggie stood with her arms crossed at the front room window of her small two room wooden house staring outside at the water drum. The white cloth tied around its top was brown from dust and the dry tree leaves that had gathered. It had been three weeks since it had rained, and the dry season along with other things was starting to affect her and her daughter, Sarah.

Sarah was a soft-spoken tiny girl of eight. She was a honey colour, and was nicknamed Picks. Her father gave her the name because she was always moving her fingers back and forth in her plaited short hair as if she was picking something.

Picks lived with her mother in Harbour Hill Community. It was a small community by the sea situated on a small hill facing inland. Scattered haphazardly down and across the hill was a mix of Caribbean wooden houses bordered by vegetable gardens, trees and bushes. The houses were designed with slanted zinc roofs, wooden double doors and windows.

Some had a cistern on the outside with a spout attached to it from the roof, while other houses had water drums. Some houses were weathered, and others were colourful – painted blue, yellow, beige and green. On the flat area at the bottom of the hill was the community main road, houses, a water well, an open field for community activities, and a small shop that sold groceries. Many dirt and bush paths running up and down the hill connected the houses. The community was quiet on most days, but if you were passing through you would see people cooling out under a tree off the main road having a lively discussion in their small groups. It was a peaceful community where no-one ever locked his door.

Aggie had an old weathered house located at the bottom of the hill. She was a tall slender young woman of smooth dark complexion who always wore her shoulder-length wavy black hair back in a pony tail. She was affable, and she believed that manners maketh the man.

When she woke up that morning, she put on a red t-shirt and brown flared skirt, but she didn't bother combing her hair, so she put on a black head tie, and went to the front room and opened the window and stood there.

Sarah came from the bedroom wearing a short green polyester frock stretching her thin arms, and walked to where her mother stood and said, 'Good morning ma.' Aggie said nothing. She was deep in thought. Sarah rubbed her eyes, then stepped over to the table and lifted the top off the bucket of drinking water. She wanted water to wash her face, but it was almost empty. She left and went into the yard and sat on a rock under the almond tree, and started moving her fingers back and forth in her hair. When the wind blew, the sound of the dry leaves rattling reminded her of rain drops on their wooden house. She thought, I wish it could rain so my mother would be happy.

As the morning sun gleamed through the house, Aggie continued to stare out the window. She needed water for the house, the food box was empty, the lamp wick was burning on the fumes, and Sarah's father was away working on another island called St. Kitts. He worked in the cane fields and he always sent money by post every week, but nothing had come since two weeks ago, and only a few cents was left in the money pan. She'd asked around the community if anyone had heard news about her partner. But no one had.

'Sarah, Sarah,' Aggie called, as her tall slender frame strolled across the room from the window to the front door, 'Come inside, I want you to go and give Mr. Fleming a message.'

Mr. Fleming was an older man who lived with his wife at the bottom of the hill, a few houses across from Sarah's mother house. He gave them drinking water, and he had a pickup truck that he used to transport water to the neighbours from the community well.

Sarah stood by the front door while her mother leaned over onto the kitchen table and wrote the message. When Aggie was finished she folded the note and handed it to Sarah. 'Take this to Mr. Fleming, and mind your manners and say good morning, please and thank you when required. Wait for his reply and come straight back home. I need to know what he says.' Aggie put her hand across her forehead. 'Your mother feels weak and has a slight headache and must lie down, so go and hurry back home.'

'Okay ma,' Sarah said. And she was off barefoot through the dirt path to Mr. Fleming's house.

Mr. Fleming had a three room house with a cistern and a porch. The walls were painted beige and the wooden windows and doors were painted sunshine yellow. When Sarah arrived into the yard, Mr. Fleming was sitting on the porch with his wife shelling peas.

'Good morning Mr. and Mrs. Fleming my mother sends this message.' 'Good morning,' they replied.

She handed the note to Mr. Fleming and he told her to give it to Mrs. Fleming that she would tell him what it says. Mrs. Fleming took the note and opened it and held it out a foot and a half away from her eyes and started reading. While she was reading, Mr. Fleming asked Sarah how her mother was doing. Sarah told him that she had a headache and was lying down. Mrs. Fleming interrupted. 'Aggie wants to go the water well. She asked if you're going tomorrow. They don't have any water.'

'My truck isn't working,' Mr. Fleming said in a regretful tone. 'Tell her I'm sorry I can't make it, but I believe Gary might be going. Tell her to ask him.'

Mrs. Fleming went into the house and grabbed a piece of paper and wrote it down in a note. She called out to Sarah and told her to come into the living room. 'Take this note to your mother and tell her if she needs water to drink she can come by at anytime. Would you like a Johnny cake? I baked them this morning.'

'Yes! Thank you Mrs. Fleming.'

Mrs. Fleming went into the kitchen and came back with a couple of things in her hand and said, 'Take one of the Johnny cakes for your mother and give her this small bag of flour. Tell her I hope she feels better and I hope she gets Gary to take her to the well.'

'Thank you Mrs. Fleming.'

They both went back on to the porch, and Mrs. Fleming joined her husband and carrying on shelling peas.

'Go straight back home to your mother now,' Mr. Fleming said.

'I will, thank you, Mr. and Mrs. Fleming. Bye, bye.' Sarah said as she waved.

She was off back through the dirt path eating her Johnny cake. When she got home she called out to her mother, but no answer. She looked in the bed room and her mother was on the bed resting. She put the Johnny cake, bag of flour and the note on the kitchen table, and then went into the yard and sat on a rock moving her fingers back and forth in her hair and thought about how she could help her mother get water. While she was sitting, her friend Carol who lived next door came by and asked if she wanted to come by her house to play ladder.

'We can play but in my yard. My mother is resting and I have to give her a message when she wakes up.'

Carol drew a long ladder in the dirt with many box shapes. Carol played first. She took her slippers off and threw a marble into a box and hopped to where it landed picked it up and hopped back. They got excitable when Sarah lost her balance and fell over while hopping.

'Sarah I told you I have a headache can you play quietly?' Aggie said as she stuck her head out of the bedroom window. 'Come inside and tell me what Mr. Fleming said. Hello Carol, how are you?'

'Good morning Miss Aggie,' Carol said. 'I'm good.'

Sarah went in the house and gave her mother the note and the Johnny cake and flour. 'Did you thank Mr. and Mrs. Fleming?' Aggie asked

'Yes I did ma. I'm sorry your head still hurts, and Mrs. Fleming said she hopes you feel better.'

'Maybe I'll feel better after I eat this Johnny cake,' Aggie said as she opened the note. She and read it and said, 'I need you to take a message to Gary.'

'Ma, can I go to the well and help get the water?'

'You are too young my dear and you can't lift a bucket full of water.'

'But I want to help. I wish for the rain to come so you don't feel sad that we don't have any water.'

Aggie said, 'Come here and give me a hug. I'll tell you what I'm going to do.' She wrote the message while saying to Sarah, 'I'm going to ask Gary to take you to the well tomorrow, and if his girl friend is going I'll ask if she could look out for you to make sure you wash your skin and hair; that way we'll have water for an extra day. Now, take this note to Gary, and Sarah, remember to mind your manners.'

'Okay ma,' she said with joy in her voice, pleased that she was going to help her mother get water.

Sarah was off barefoot through a bush path to Gary's house taking Carol with her this time. Gary was a young man, who lived at the top of the hill in a two room wooden house similar to Aggie's house, but his house had a cistern and it was painted sky blue all round. When the girls arrived, his girlfriend Eve was in the yard hanging out clothes. She was shapely, and was wearing a short pant and t-shirt, with the clothes pins pinned on her t-shirt.

'Good mornings Miss Eve,' the girls said breathing fast.

'Howdy girls,' Eve said as she took a pin from her t-shirt and pinned a shirt on to the clothes line. 'I can see you both tired from walking up this hill.'

'My mother sends this for Gary,' Sarah said, handing her the note.

Eve dried her hands on her t-shirt, took the note and put in her pants pocket, and told Sarah Gary wasn't home.

'Miss Eve, can Carol and I have some water to drink please?'

'Give me a minute to finish here and I'll get you girls some water. Go and wait in the shade under the Neem tree.'

While the girls were waiting, Sarah saw a small bucket with a handle that had clothes pins in it at the side of the house where Eve was washing her clothes. She thought if she had one of those she could carry water home to her mother. She imagined if she had her own bucket she would go to the well and get water every day and they would always have water.

Eve came over and went into the house and got both girls a cup of water. Carol slowly drank her water, but Sarah put the cup to her mouth until it was empty. She handed the cup back to Eve and said. 'Miss Eve where did you get that little bucket you have the clothes pin in? I want one.'

'You mean the paint bucket?'

Sarah nodded her head.

'Gary gets them from other people when they finished painting. We also use them to bucket the water out of the cistern. He has a few at the back.'

'Can I have one, please Miss Eve, can I have one? I want to carry water in it for my mother.'

'I'll ask Gary if you can have one.'
Picks was a bit disappointed because she wanted to take it home with her now.

Eve looked at Picks and said, 'You want to show your mother that you are becoming a hard working young lady by having your own bucket to carry water?'

Sarah smiled shyly and nodded her head.

'Off you go now, your mother is probably wondering where you are all this time, and say hello to her for me.'

Both girls say bye to Eve, and were walking out of the yard when Sarah stopped and said, 'Thank you Miss Eve for the water you gave Carol and me.' Sarah was so caught up in getting her bucket that she forgot her manners. She knew her mother would not stand for her not saying her manners, and would make her go back and say them.

Eve said, 'okay,' and waved goodbye. She stood under the Neem tree and watched until the girls disappeared down the hill through the bush path. She thought about how Picks wanted to get her own bucket so she could carry water for her mother. She thought about how hard times make children more responsible at an early age. She then went back to finish hanging out the rest of her clothes.

When Sarah went into the house her mother was raking out the last remaining butter from the tin to put in the Johnny cake. She told her what Eve said, and then went outside to carrying on playing ladder. She threw her marble and she hopped into the first box.

'Sarah,' Aggie called. 'Stop playing and go across on the land and pick some limes so I can make limeade to drink with this Johnny cake.'

Carol heard what Aggie said and left. Sarah went into the house and grabbed a little plastic bowl, when Aggie said, 'Be careful with the prickly lime bush, and watch your step around the lime tree, so you don't get any prickles in your foot.'

'I will ma.' And she was off to pick limes. While picking limes she heard a vehicle drive into the yard. She started picking the limes fast and her finger got caught on a prickle. It gave a little tingle, but it didn't bleed, so she filled up the bowl and hurried back to the house to see who it was. It was Gary, and her mother was looking into the back of his pickup truck.

'Howdy, Picks,' Gary said, leaning over the back of his pickup truck wearing a faded red sports cap on his head. 'Eve said you came by so I stop by to tell your mom to be ready early because I'm leaving 7 in the morning to go the water well. What you have there?'

'Limes.'

Aggie looked at Sarah and said, 'Aren't you going to ask Gary if he want some limes? Look he has fish in his truck that he caught this morning and he scaled and gutted them. He has Hines, Doctor and Butter fish; he said we can have a few.'

Gary lowered the truck's tailgate as Sarah walked over. She looked at the fish on a plastic bag spread out on the floor of the pickup truck and said to herself, There are small fish.

'Come here and give me some of those limes,' Gary said, 'Eve love fresh lime juice on her fish.'

Sarah handed out the bowl and he took a few while Aggie picked out a few fish from the truck. She put them in a bag she took from Gary's truck and gave it to Sarah. Sarah took them to the back and put it on the outside table, and carried the limes in the house. Aggie thanked Gary and told him she'll have Sarah ready tomorrow. And Gary drove off.

Aggie went into the house and made limeade and Sarah went in the front yard and sat on her rock under the almond tree moving her fingers back and forth in her hair. She wondered if Eve had told Gary about the bucket, because he didn't bring her a bucket.

Aggie poured two cups and took them outside, handed a cup to Sarah and sat down beside her. She gave Sarah a piece of her Johnny cake and Sarah smiled and said, 'Thank you ma.'

Aggie looked at her and said, 'you really helped me today; I have a lot on my mind.'

Sarah was chewing a piece of Johnny cake when she thought, if my father was home my mother wouldn't have a lot on her mind because he helps with everything. She looked at her mother and asked. 'When is pa coming home?'

Aggie wasn't sure how to answer Sarah, so she said in a funny voice, 'Eat your Johnny cake and drink your limeade before the bugs come and get it.' They both laughed and carried on eating.

After Aggie finished her meal she went into the house and started sweeping the floor. Her headache had disappeared and she was feeling energetic. She seasoned the fish with salt to cook later for their evening meal. Then she called out to Sarah, 'Come inside, the sun is getting hot.' Sarah got up and went inside, and the two took an afternoon nap.

The sun had cooled down when Aggie woke from her nap. With the flour Mrs. Fleming sent, she started preparing the dough for Johnny cakes. After she had finished, she went into the bedroom and told Sarah who was still lying in bed to go into the cob, get some wood and put it in the outdoor fire place and wait for her to come and light it. Sarah got up and fetched the wood. She was placing them neatly in the fire place when Aggie came outside with a piece of brown paper and matches in her hand and said, 'Get some dry leaves. I need them to help get the fire light.' Sarah got the dry leaves from the almond tree. Aggie placed them and the paper under the wood and lit it. Sarah stood back and watched the wood burning in a small blaze, and Aggie went back into the house and put the Johnny cakes in the baking pan.

When the blaze was lowered, Aggie put the Johnny cakes to bake and the fish to fry. Sarah stayed and fetched more wood as needed, and Aggie checked on the cooking.

Before the sun set, they both sat down under the almond tree and ate their meal. After they had eaten, Aggie went into the house and poured the last of the remaining drinking water in a tub to wipe off their skin before bed. Then she went to Mr. Flemings and got a bucket of drinking water. They both had an early night.

The following morning, when Gary arrived, Aggie and Sarah were waiting in their yard with four big buckets. They loaded them on to the pickup truck alongside the many buckets that were already there. Eve, who was also sitting in the front of the truck stuck her head out the window and said, 'Come Picks, sit in the front with us.' Aggie walked with her to the front of the truck, and gave her a little paper bag; in it was soap and a small cloth. She said, 'Be good and helpful. Do what your elders say.' Sarah said 'Yes ma.' She then hopped into the truck, climbed over Eve and sat in the middle. Gary eased his foot off the brakes and said 'We have to go.' As the truck drove away leaving a thin cloudy trace of dust, Sarah waved to her mother and she waved back. Aggie stood in the yard until the truck was no longer visible.

The buckets banged against each other as Gary drove along the community road. 'I hope there aren't a lot of people at the well,' he said, steadily increasing the pickup truck's speed. 'I want to get back to make some fish pots before the sun gets too hot.'

'Would I get my bucket filled with water and would I have time to wash my hair and scrub my skin?' Picks asked.

'Yes you would.' Gary answered.

They got to the well and just what he feared was present; people were washing and people waiting with their buckets to get water.

At the well was a big tamarind tree where everyone cooled out while waiting to fill up their buckets. Gary parked the truck and started taking the buckets out. He called out to Picks, 'Come and see what I found in one of my buckets. She ran over and looked in the bucket, and there was a little paint bucket all cleaned and ready for her to carry water. She grabbed the handle and lifted it out and said with excitement, 'Thank you Gary, my mother is going to be happy.' Gary took all the buckets and joined the waiting line.

Picks swung her bucket from her hand as Eve and she walked to the Tamarind tree. They sat down under the tree and Eve helped her loosen out her plaits. And they watched as women placed a full bucket of water on a wrapped cloth on their heads and some walked home without holding the bucket. Picks like seeing them do that, but knew she was too young to try it. She thought, she would try it one day with her little bucket, though.

Gary waved his hand to Eve as to say come fast it's our turn. Eve and Picks walked over to the well where Gary was just starting to fill up a bucket with water, and Picks put her little bucket in the row. Eve told Picks to take one of her big buckets to Gary, and he filled it up. Eve took the bucket of water behind the tree for Picks and said, 'Hurry up and scrub your body and wash your hair. Gary needs the bucket to fill it up.'

Picks looked in the bucket of water and said, 'I don't have anything to throw the water over my body.'

'Your mother didn't put one in the bucket?'

Picks shrugged her shoulders and said, 'I don't know.'

'I'll go and look; maybe she put it in one of the other buckets.'

Picks took off her dress and scooped out the water with her hands, soaped her cloth and started scrubbing her skin. Eve came back with the bottom half of a plastic soda bottle she got from someone at the well, and gave it to Picks who was covered in soap suds. She then went back to the well and took over from Gary, and he started carrying a bucket in each hand and loaded them on to the truck. They were working fast.

Picks came from behind the tree with water running down her face from her hair swinging the bucket, when Gary said. 'Make haste and bring the bucket.' She picked up her pace and took it to him. He filled it up, loaded it on to the truck and they were on their way home.

Picks was feeling good. She'd gotten her own bucket, a full body scrub and she knew her mother was going to be happy because they'll have water for the next few days.

Gary drove up into her yard. Picks climbed over Eve out of the truck into the yard running toward the door with excitement in her voice calling, 'ma, ma I'm back; we have water and I got my own bucket.' Just as she reached to the front door her father came and stood in the door and she jumped into his arms. 'Pa, when did you get back?'

He held her in his arms and said, 'my little Picks, I see you've been helping your mother.'

'Yes, I went to the well and got water for ma so she could be happy, and I have my own bucket so I can always go to the well and get water.'

While the two embraced, Gary came out of the truck and shook his hand and said, 'good to see you man, but I have to deliver the rest of the water to our neighbours.' Her dad took the buckets from the truck, and thanked Gary and Eve.

Picks said to her father to look, she wanted to show him she could carry a bucket of water. She picked up her bucket full of water and started walking leaned to one side spilling the water. After a few steps she switched the bucket to her other hands still spilling the water. Her father took the bucket off her and said 'I'll put the buckets to the back; you're getting strong.' He then held Picks' little hand and they went into the house. Her mother was standing at the kitchen table taking food from a bag and putting it in the food box with a warm smile on her face. 'Ma, I have my own bucket and pa is back,' Sarah said, still with excitement in her voice. 'Did he bring food?'

'Yes my dear, and you brought water. I have all that I need, and you helped make it happened.'

The end

Denise Crawford

Sightseeing in Island Harbour Village

If you are spending your holiday with us or planning a day trip to the village, there is a lot to see and explore. Most sights are along the village main road and are easy to find. If you would like to visit the Big Spring heritage site you'd have to organize a tour with the Anguilla National Trust.

St. Andrews Anglican church is a great sight to see and a good starting point for your tour. A short drive from the church will take you to the art gallery on lower Island Harbour bay. After that, you can continue on to the main hub of the bay. All parking is free, so you can drive from attraction to attraction. A walk along our crescent-shaped beach will not disappoint. There, you'll see our beach school, traditional island houses, Arawak Inn and sea-side nature. Hopefully you'll be having lunch with us. Everett's is at the main hub and it's a great spot to cool down and enjoy a drink and get some local food. After lunch, admire the sea views as you drive east towards the Broad Path community that takes you into Harbour Ridge community. While there, be sure to stop off and browse around Hibernia restaurant and art gallery. Then proceed further east to Captain's Ridge sea-side community until you reach an area where you'll see Captain Bay beach, Scrub Island, and the entire village and sea views near and far. Stop off and immerse yourself in one of the most magnificent views on the island. The low-lying limestone scrubby land along with the view is worth the drive up to Captain's Ridge. And before you finish your tour, take a short drive to East End Village and visit Anguilla's Cultural Museum and the Old East End Primary School. They are just yards apart, and you'll also see the pond that hindered some of us getting to school back in the day.

Now you have returned to Island Harbour, ready to take your shoes off and enjoy a drink. You can end your day with a stop off at On de Rocks for some late afternoon cocktails sitting upstairs in the restaurant feeling the fresh cool breeze while admiring our finest asset – the harbour with its colourful boats with Scilly Cay and the surrounding areas in the near distance. If you are coming back for dinner, the Arawak Inn and Hibernia won't disappoint.

Island Harbour Village